GUIDE
TO
CONSUMER RIGHTS

DAVID MARSH
EASYWAY GUIDES

1

Easyway Guides
38 Cromwell Road, London E17 9JN

Straightforward Publishing
First Edition 1997

British Library cataloguing in Publication Data. A catalogue record is available for this book from the British Library.

ISBN 1 900694 45 X

Printed by BPC Wheaton Ltd, Exeter.
Cover Design by Straightforward Graphics.

GUIDE TO THE RIGHTS OF THE CONSUMER

CONTENTS

4

INTRODUCTION

This book is a brief overview of consumer rights and has been written both for the general public and also for the student of the law as it governs the consumer.

The aim of the book is to outline the rights of the consumer when entering into a transaction with a seller of goods. Many people do not know their rights when encountering problems at the point of sale or after. What , for example, are your rights if goods turn out to be unsuitable or substandard and the seller refuses to let you have your money back or generally try's to tell you that there is nothing that can be done.

Another area which causes problems is that of consumer credit. Many people are taken in by what seem, on the face of it, to be favourable terms. However, the small print is rarely read and problems ensue.

Hire agreements are also covered along with the sale of unsafe goods. Food safety and general hygiene are also outlined.

The rights of the consumer are quite considerable and yet most of us live in complete ignorance of exactly what they are. The obligations upon the shopkeeper and those who sell us goods generally are considerable, corresponding with consumer rights.

The primary purpose of this book is to educate the consumer and to empower him/her by fostering an understanding of the responsibilities of the seller. The responsibilities of the consumer in relation to transactions will also be pointed out.

It is hoped that all will benefit by reading this book. The rights of the consumer are of paramount importance and it is one area where general education leaves a lot to be desired.

CHAPTER ONE

THE RIGHTS OF THE CONSUMER GENERALLY

All consumer transactions are based on the law of contract. Following on from this, every exchange of goods is an agreement between buyer and seller.

However, underpinning each exchange is an area of law which defines the rights and obligations of buyer and seller. The purchaser and the person who sells are not free to do exactly as they wish after the sale or, indeed, make up the rules as they go along, which seems to be the situation in a lot of cases.

The major area of law, which supports and assists consumers is the *Sale of Goods Act 1979*. This Act governs all transactions where goods are transferred for a price.

There are certain situations where a consumer will not be covered by the Sale of Goods Act. As was mentioned, this Act covers transactions where money is involved, where a price has been set for the goods. For example, in some circumstances you may swap or exchange goods. In this case, the transaction will be governed by the *Supply of Goods and Services Act 1982*. We will discuss this a little later.

There are a number of transactions which may involve a combination of swap and cash, such as the trading in of a product against a newer model. If an amount of cash is involved, no matter how small, then the Sale of Goods Act 1979 will apply.

The contract of sale

There are what is known as **"express and implied"** conditions governing any contract, not just consumer contracts. Express terms of the contract are those agreed by the buyer and seller. However, once it has been determined that the Sale of Goods Act covers the transaction there are certain conditions implied into the sale by the Act. These conditions cannot be circumvented by the seller.

Description

In every contract for the Sale of Goods, the 1979 Act states that where there is a sale of goods by description there is simultaneously an implied condition that the goods sold will match their description. In other words, the seller must sell you what has been described in the advertising. Nothing more and nothing less will suffice.

Example

A shopkeeper advertises paint which leads the potential buyer to believe that it is a leading brand. There is nothing in the advertising to indicate that the situation may be otherwise. However, when you are about to hand over the money, you realise that the paint is not that brand but something which is similar but of questionable quality.

This is a common situation and relies a lot on the power of advertising. However, as has been seen the shopkeeper has an obligation under the Sale Of Goods Act 1979 to sell what has been advertised, or to sell goods which correspond to the description of them.

Section 13 of the Sale of Goods Act applies to all sales, whether by private individuals or business. Anyone who sells a good to another is covered.

Section 13 applies to all goods no matter what the purchasing situation. Just because, for example, the goods were on open display and the potential buyer can see what is on offer, does not mean that sale by description does not apply. A tin of fruit might contain a different fruit to what is described in the tin or a sweater might in fact not be 100 per cent wool as it says on the label.

The golden rule which underpins the Act is that the description of the product on offer must match the product sold.

As television shopping assumes greater prominence, in the form of television shopper channels, this Act will assume greater importance. No longer will there be the direct face to face contact between the buyer and the seller, only a telephone line. The process of challenging the product when you eventually receive it will be more long winded, as it often is

with mail order of whatever description. However, consumers will need to be aware of their rights in the probable instance of receiving goods that do not correspond to what was requested.

Samples

There may be cases where the consumer purchases goods and relies on a sample to make a choice. This is quite often the case when choosing fabric for furnishings or carpets. The Sale of Goods Act also covers samples and states that the goods must correspond with the description of those goods and not just the sample shown. This is very important for those who feel let down by goods received by way of choosing from sample and wish to return those goods.

Remember *THE SALE OF GOODS ACT 1979 SECTION 13* is the Act that you should refer to if you experience problems in this area.

Your rights under this section entitle you to reject the goods and obtain a refund. It is not at the discretion of the seller, but your right.

In addition to the goods not matching up to the description, section 30 of the Act also provides a remedy to the consumer if **quantity** of goods is not that which was requested or advertised. Quite simply, because a different amount is supplied then there has been a breach of description.

If the consumer receives a mixture of goods, for example, two saucepans ordered but the third different to the one described then the right exists to reject the goods. There is no right for the consumer to keep the goods. They must be returned if rejected.

When items purchased are defective

We have all been in the situation where we have purchased something, got home and found it to be defective. In most cases, we can confidently assume that goods can be returned and exchanged or money refunded. However, this is not always the case and sometimes the seller will make life difficult, even going so far as to refuse to exchange goods or refund money.

This is a blatant breach of the law and of the rights of the consumer. Again, it is necessary to be able to quote the law at such people and show that you mean business.

There are many examples of defective goods. This can range from the washing machine or fridge to the item of clothing that either has a defect or does not last the first wash.

The Sale of Goods Act 1979 covers these situations. The seller has to be an established business however. It is most important to understand this point. The Act does not cover private sales. However, the purchaser can be business or private. There is no distinction here.

Merchantable Quality

Goods sold in the course of business must be what is known as "of merchantable quality. Section 14 of the Sale of Goods Act defines this. Basically, goods are of a merchantable quality if they are as fit for the purpose for which goods of that kind are commonly bought. In other words, the good must be the same high quality as other goods of a similar kind. If they are not then they are defective.

Defective goods and repairs

Sometimes you buy a good, find that it is defective, take it back and are told by the salesman that it can be repaired quite easily. What is your position then? The position is that you do not have to accept a repair to the item but can demand an exchange or refund. However, there will be cases where the repairing of an item is the only way forward from a practical point of view. This is quite reasonable in the circumstances.

Sometimes, and this is quite common, a guarantee will be given with a product. This gives the consumer an automatic right to a replacement if a good is defective.

Second hand goods

The situation is slightly different when the consumer purchases a second hand item. The same condition applies as to new goods but obviously age and condition of the item have to be taken into account and the buyer should realise that there is a greater risk of a defect. However, the Sale of Goods Act still applies in the case of second hand goods.

There is one proviso here. That is that the Sale of Goods Act says that goods must be of merchantable quality unless the defect is pointed out to the buyer by the seller. Examination of the goods, and the acceptance of those goods provides a get out for many sellers.

This situation can be awkward as many buyers are keen to examine anything they buy. If you miss a defect in a good then the seller has the right to say that you should have noticed the defect. In many cases, of Course, the defect may not be readily apparent. If you do examine goods before purchase then it is highly advisable to check thoroughly before acceptance.

Fitness for purpose

The Sale of Goods Act section 14 also governs what is known as "fitness for purpose". Fitness for purpose quite simply means that the goods purchased must be reasonably fit for the purpose for which they are made. For example, a purchase of a dishwashing machine would lead us to believe that we are buying something that can wash dishes. If this is not the case then the consumer has every right to return the goods.

There are examples here, though, where the buyer cannot demand recompense from the seller if he has not relied on the skill and judgement of the seller. A typical example may be where the buyer goes into a shop and demands something that he assumes is compatible with something else, for example, a printer which he asks for by name, receives it and subsequently finds that it is not fit for the purpose. The key is to ask as many questions as possible before purchasing in order to give the seller as much information as is needed to ensure that the good that he is selling is the correct good.

Buyers of goods

Buyers of goods have to understand the nature and consequences of *acceptance of goods.*

The Sale of Goods Act sections 34 and 35 deal with acceptance. Section 35 is very important. Basically, if a buyer accepts goods then any damages payable on subsequently discovering a problem will be affected.

Acceptance of a good or goods is recognised to occur in a number of ways. One such way is by intimation. This can occur when a buyer or business does not inspect goods, signs for them and only after discovers problems. There are acts after delivery which are not consistent with the sellers ownership. This is usually more important in commercial rather than straightforward consumer cases. If the buyer retains the goods beyond what is considered a reasonable time then this can constitute acceptance and can undermine the case for compensation.

It is true to say that most consumers would not look for damages if the good that they have purchased is defective in one way or another. Usually the act of replacing or repairing a good is seen as fair and equitable.

Other consumer transactions and the law

We have looked at transactions between seller and buyer which are covered by the Sale of Goods Act. However, there are transactions which are not covered by the Act, simply because there is no "transfer of property for a monetary consideration called a price".

An example may be the purchase of a good under a hire purchase agreement. We will be discussing this in more depth later. However, purchase of goods in this way constitutes "bailment". In other words, the goods are owned by the hire purchase company until the last payment is made. If the good is defective in this case, what is the remedy?

Hire purchase transactions of this kind are covered by the *Supply of Goods (implied terms) Act 1973*. Sections 9 and 10 are exactly the same as sections 13 and 14 of the Sale of Goods Act and therefore the remedy lies here.

There is another form of consumer transaction which needs to be understood. This is known as the *conditional sale transaction*. This is where a buyer of a good, a typical example being a car, may have the car for six months and have constant trouble. If the buyer experiences ongoing trouble and the garage is alerted then he will be entitled to a refund of his money.

There is an important point to be made here. That is the buyers attitude and whether or not he accepts the good even though it is defective. Two notions exist-**acceptance and affirmation**. What this means is that **acceptance** will occur when the buyer accepts delivery. However, **affirmation** can only occur when the defect is known, with time starting to run from that point. If the buyer simply carries on driving the car, or using the good even though there is knowledge of the defect then he is accepting the good and undermining his right to return or seek compensation. However, if the buyer does not affirm, i.e., continually lets the garage know that there has been problems, then he is not affirming the contract and will be entitled to a refund.

Be very careful here. Always assert your right, do not be afraid of complaining and keep a record of the number of times that you have complained.

Use of materials when carrying out repairs

Responsibility, or liability, for parts under a contract which is for works and materials is regulated by sections 3 and 4 of part 1 of the Supply of

Goods and Services Act 1973. If a remedy is needed for the supply of parts which are either defective or are not those which are supposed to have been used then it is to this Act that you must turn. As before, the notion of affirmation and acceptance is of paramount importance.

When it comes to the service element of a contract, as opposed to the materials element, then it is to section 13 of the Supply of Goods and Services Act that you must turn. Section 13 states that work must be carried out with reasonable care and skill.

There are other terms implied into a service contract. Section 14 implies that the business doing the servicing must carry it out within a reasonable time. This is where there are no express terms in the agreement. In addition, section 15 indicates that where no price has been agreed then a reasonable price must be agreed. A reasonable price is one which another company would charge for the same work.

Therefore, if you feel that you are being overcharged then you can challenge it, underpinned by the backing of section 15 of the Goods and Services Act. There is one very important rider here. That is if the supplier has quoted a high price and the consumer has accepted then there can be no redress, not even if you find that another company will provide that service for far less.

CONSUMER BEWARE. Always shop around. If you feel that the price is too high then ask elsewhere. Always try to avoid entering into an agreement with no stated price.

Of course, there will always be the case where it is not really possible to get a price. This is where protection under section 15 comes in.

Example

You discover that you are receiving electric shocks off your car. You telephone a local garage that specialises in car electric's and the owner tells you to "drop your car in". You do this and telephone the garage later to see what the problem is. The garage owner informs you that the problem was minor, with a power lead earthing. The problem has been rectified and you can collect the car. You do this and you are informed that the bill is £150. Quite rightly, you think that this is too high. Two things can happen here, and often do. On one hand the garage owner can tell you that that is what he charges and you must pay it. The other is that you can find out what an alternative garage would pay for the same work and establish a reasonable price, refusing to go above this.

The problem that you have to sort out here is how to get your car back. You have to argue the case with the garage and let them know that you understand your rights as a consumer and you have read and understood the law that governs this particular problem.

It is the case that when businesses realise that they may get bad publicity and the person in front of them knows their rights , they generally back down, as it is bad for business.

If there has been a breach of services contract then the normal solution or remedy is damages to put the defective or poor work right. Damages for distress or disappointment can be awarded in some cases although there are certain areas where it is difficult, such as holidays.

The Consumer Protection Act 1987

The above Act covers those instances where a person has been injured because of a defective good. This Act also covers the many instances where someone may have been injured or affected who is not the principal purchaser. The Consumer Protection Act therefore imposes a very strict liability for defective goods on someone who is deemed to be the producer of the product. The Act provides, or at least seeks to provide a route for the consumer to seek redress against the person who is ultimately responsible for the damage. This gets rid, or at least minimises the requirement to have to prove fault, which in the past has proven very time consuming and difficult and also very expensive.

The Act is only relevant where the consumer has purchased a defective product which has caused damage. It is essential to determine who is liable, and the Act says that the following are primarily liable for damages:

a) the producer

b) an own brander who has held himself to be the producer of a particular good

c) the first importer into the European Community. Therefore, strict liability will attach to any person or company who presents its/his self as producer of a good.

Only in a few cases will the supplier of a good be liable. These cases are limited to instances where it may not be possible to identify the producer or anyone else within or further up the chain, in a reasonable period of time.

Definition of product

It is necessary to define product. This is because some goods and services are more readily identifiable than others as products. Section 1(2) of the Consumer Protection Act defines product and has wide definitions. For example, goods include electricity. Section 45 also defines goods produced from the land, such as crops, and also other goods such as aircraft vehicles etc. A product, however, is a common sense notion and for the purposes of the every day consumer a product is fairly obvious.

A defective product is simply where the safety of the product is in question and can be a manufacturing defect, a design defect and a defect that has arisen because of a misleading warning notice. In this latter instance, this means a notice that has failed to advise the consumer how to use a product properly.

A consumer can sue under the Consumer Protection Act (s5) for:

Death caused as a result of a defective product;

Personal injury caused as a result of a defective product:

Damage to private property, above a certain sum, caused as a result of a defective product.

There is no liability for any damage to the product itself or for the loss of, or any damage to, the whole or any part of any product which has been supplied with the main product.

There are cases where, even if a manufacturer is liable under the Act, the Act contains what is known as strict liability and not absolute liability. This means that there are a number of defences that can be used by manufacturers. It is up to the defendant, i.e., the manufacturer to prove one of the following as a defence:

a) The defect was caused by the need to comply with the law as it stands at that time. This may have been the need to comply with new legislation that has recently been introduced;

b) The manufacturer did not supply the product in question-this can relate to instances of theft;

c) That the supplier of the good is not in business and is a private individual. Remember, the aim of the Act is to impose strict liability on commercial producers and it is not really the intention, or the spirit of the Act to impose any liability on individuals as such. However, individuals who are not in business are not ruled out;

d) That the defect did not exist in the product at the time of supply. One very good example has been the recent spate of contaminating certain products as they lie on shelves, such a baby food and also chocolate. If contamination takes place in the shop then it is important to note that the seller, or retailer becomes liable under the Sale of Goods Act;

e) Another defence, perhaps the most complicated and controversial is that of the state of scientific (and technical) knowledge at the time was not such that a producer of products of the same description as the product in question might be expected to have discovered. Here, a producer of a product has to demonstrate that at the time in question they could not be expected to know of the defect;

f) Finally, that the producer of a component part of a product had produced a defective product and the defect was as a result of instructions given by the main producer.

A consumer may bring a claim against a manufacturer within a certain timescale-in relation to personal injuries or any damage to property there is a three year time period within which to bring a claim. However, as far as a manufacturer of a product is concerned, there is a 10 year cut off point from the time that a particular product was supplied to a retailer.

There are some instances where a recall notice may be issued by a manufacturer to a retailer. This is happening all the time, in the cases of baby food, cars and other items. This in no way relieves the manufacturer of liability although it can certainly help to reduce the amount of compensation gained by an aggrieved person.

Notices that attempt to deny, or exclude liability for product

We have all seen notices on products which say that the manufacturer is excluded from all liability for a good. This is a very important area and we need to look at the actual liability of a manufacturer even if an exclusion notice has been given. There is nothing stopping a shopkeeper or manufacturer from stonewalling your claim for damages due to the fact that an exclusion notice has been attached to a product.

Typical exclusion notices might read:

"No responsibility will be accepted for goods once they have left the store"

"There will be no refund for this good, even if found to be unsuitable"

"We accept no returns under any circumstances"

The list is endless and can apply to a whole range of products. However, what the consumer needs to know is whether a retailer can actually impose any of these restrictions. Can a retailer avoid the liabilities imposed under the Sale of Goods Act or the Supply of Goods Act or any other Act?

There is one major starting point for all exclusion notices. What we need to determine is whether or not the notice has been incorporated, or is an integral part of, the contract for sale. If this has not occurred then there can be no exclusion notice. Incorporation means that if a consumer signs a contract they are bound by it, in the absence of any sort of misrepresentation. So, if a consumer has signed a contract they are bound by its terms. However, if the terms are contained in an unsigned document which is an exclusion notice, the terms will only form part of the actual contract if there has been an attempt to bring the notice to the consumers attention.

The Unfair Contract Terms Act 1977 is of importance in determining whether or not a consumer has signed an unfair, or onerous contract. The Act will govern any clause which purports or attempts to restrict liability. The Act governs business and will control the acts of a person who, through contract, attempts to deny any liability for a good where there in fact does exist a liability in law.

As we have seen so far there are a range of laws which protect the consumer and place obligations on manufacturers and suppliers. Merely to insert an exclusion clause, thereby giving full protection against the law, is an absurdity.

In practice, the unfair Contract Terms Act operates in three areas:

a) Where there are exclusions in relation to the implied terms section of the Sale of Goods Act 1979 and the 1982 Sale of Goods Act (implied Terms).

b) The person supplying the goods is trying to avoid negligence based liability;

c) The person supplying the goods is trying to avoid liability for any other breach of contract.

Example

A removal firm undertakes to do a job for Mr and Mrs Smith. They inform the couple that their liability for any damages to goods is covered by an exclusion clause in a contract that they wish to sign. This states that liability for any damage is limited to £35 per item or £100 in total.

Can they do this? What they are trying to do is to avoid the above Acts which impose liabilities for negligence and the answer would be no, they cannot limit their own liability.

A very important point to note is that if you are dealing with a retailer as a consumer then the retailer cannot avoid responsibility as contained in the implied terms of contract which are governed by the Sale of Goods and Supply of Goods Acts.

There may be occasions where other goods, such as exchanged goods, hire goods or the materials part of a contract are concerned and the Supply of Goods Act (implied terms) and Sale of Goods Act do not apply. The Supply of Goods and Services Act governs these areas and section seven of the Unfair Contract Terms Act refers.

The Unfair Contract Terms Act also covers negligence based clauses, i.e., where a manufacturer denies liability for negligence. Section 1 of the Unfair Contract Terms Act defines negligence as the breach of duty of care arising in contract.

As far as the consumer is concerned, the area which is most likely to arise is an attempt to avoid liability for a breach of section 13 of the Supply of Goods and Services Act.

Section 2 of the Unfair Contract Terms Act says that any clause (or notice) is invalid in so far as it attempts to exclude liability for negligence *resulting in death or personal injury.*

Section 2(2) of the Act also goes on to state that if any other loss or damage arises as a result then the clause of the notice will only be valid provided a reasonableness test is satisfied.

The reasonableness test contains guidelines and include:

a) the strength of the bargaining position between parties to a contract

b) whether there was any inducement to agree to the term, i.e., was there any special offer or was the consumer put in a position where he/ she had to agree before purchase;

c) whether the consumer knew of any term in the first place;

d) whether the goods were specially manufactured.

The Unfair Contract Terms Act also deals with other breaches of contract such as where a business will try to exclude or restrict liability to a certain sum or claims to be entitled to give a good or service which is in fact substantially different to that stated. A common example here is that of a tour operator stating that they have the right to offer alternative holidays. The Act also covers the notice which claims to have no liability for the non delivery of a service.

Section 4 of the Act states that a person dealing as a consumer cannot be made to indemnify another person against liability for negligence or breach of contract unless the reasonableness test has been passed. Section 5 deals with manufacturers guarantees to the consumer and states that if goods which are supplied for private use or consumption prove defective whilst in use and cause loss or damage as a result of negligence in manufacture or distribution, then any attempt to avoid liability in a guarantee is void.

If misrepresentation is involved, then any attempt to exclude liability for misrepresentation is only valid provided that the reasonableness test is passed.

There are areas of law which will make it a criminal liability to give an exclusion notice. *The Consumer Transactions (Restrictions on Statements) Order 1976* as amended, makes it a criminal offence to use a void exemption clause in a contract. Therefore, a notice such as no refunds etc., can make the seller criminally liable. The order also makes it an offence to supply goods to a consumer with written exclusion notices without pointing out that a consumers statutory rights are unaffected.

The effect of the European Community and European Directives.

There are attempts to make liability for consumer goods standard throughout the European Community and there is a European Directive on unfair terms in Consumer contracts which will seek to give the consumer more power, particularly when dealing with large companies or corporations. Contracts which operate to the detriment of the consumer will not be allowed. The directive is concerned only with contracts between business and consumers. No contracts will be excluded from the directive.

Key Points from Chapter One.

* All consumer transactions are based on the law of contract

* The major area of law which supports and assists consumers is the Sale of Goods Act 1979

* In situations where there is an exchange of goods and cash, the Supply of Goods Act 1982 governs

* The Sale of Goods Act 1979 states that goods sold should match their description

* All consumers have the right to return or exchange defective goods

* Goods must be fit for the purpose for which they are intended

* The Supply of Goods and Services Act covers materials and works

* The Consumer Protection Act 1979 covers injury because of defective goods

* Notices that seek to deny or exclude liability are generally null and void

CHAPTER TWO

THE CONSUMER AND CREDIT

The most important Act   dealing with consumers and credit is the *Consumer Credit Act 1974.*

The aims of the 1974 Act are:

a) to regulate the formation, terms and enforcement of credit and hire agreements. The Act gives consumers many rights and places restraints upon the enforcement of an agreement against a consumer.

b) the Act sets up a licensing system whereby those engaged in any form of consumer credit business must be licensed.

c) the true cost of credit must be shown plus the annual rate of interest. It also controls door to door canvassing for credit.

There are a number of common types of credit agreements-*hire purchase* is one such credit arrangement.

Hire purchase, as mentioned before is the bailment of goods with the option to purchase. The consumer (debtor) purchases a good, but does not, or cannot, afford to buy outright. The actual financing is done via a finance company. Whilst all negotiations and agreements are usually done with the business directly selling you the good, it is the finance company who will own the good. The finance company bails out the good to the consumer with the option to purchase. The debtor is actually contracting with the finance company and not the seller for the purchase of the good. If the good turns out to be defective then the consumers rights under the Sale of Goods Act are exercisable against the finance company.

There is an agreement known as the *conditional sale agreement*. This is a sale of goods subject to a condition and the condition is that the property will not pass until the goods have been paid for. As in hire purchase the finance company has legal title to the goods until the last instalment is paid.

The conditional sale agreement works in the same way as a hire purchase agreement The only difference is that the transaction is governed by the Sale of Goods Act 1979 and not the Supply of Goods(implied terms) Act 1973, which also governs hire purchase.

There is a form of agreement known as a *credit sale agreement*. This situation usually occurs when a store is financing its own goods to increase sales. Under this type of agreement the goods pass to the consumer straight away as opposed to a finance company. The transaction is covered by the Sale of Goods Act . If services are being purchased then the transaction will be covered by the Supply of Goods and Services Act 1982.

Using a credit card

When the consumer uses a credit card to finance a purchase, as is often the case today, then the buyer is entering into a contract with the store to supply the goods. The consumer agrees to pay the card off and the store will obtain refund less commission from the card company.

Quite often, credit card companies will offer their own guarantee when purchasing goods and it is very important to make sure that you understand what the card company is offering.

Obtaining a loan where the loan company is connected to the supplier

In this situation, the debtor agrees to purchase goods or services from a supplier. The supplier has an arrangement with a finance company where the finance company agrees to loan all the suppliers clients money to purchase a good. The arrangement is then between the finance company and the supplier. The contract of sale and subsequent disputes between the buyer and seller are direct and governed by the Sale of Goods Act 1979.

One other situation is where the buyer obtains a personal loan to purchase a good, there is no link between the loan and the seller, in this case. The contract for the loan is between the buyer and loan company and the contract for sale is between the buyer and seller.

The examples listed above are the most common examples of consumer credit.

Definitions of credit

In order to fully understand the workings of the Consumer Credit Act we need to look at definitions of credit contained within the Act.

The definitions of credit are contained within sections 8-20 of the Act. Most of the controls and restrictions in the Act apply only to what is known as "regulated Agreements" For an agreement to be regulated it must fall within the definition of a consumer credit agreement contained in section 8 of the Act The agreement is a regulated one under section 8 as long as it is not exempted under section 16. So, in order to find out if your agreement is regulated, you have to ascertain whether or not it is exempt. If it is not exempt, it is regulated.

Section 8 sets out monetary limits. This section states that an agreement by which the creditor provides the individual (the word individual also encompasses partnerships, but not companies) with credit not exceeding £15,000 (this is changed from time to time) is regulated.

This is therefore the first factor which must be considered when determining whether an agreement is regulated. Many lenders, because of this amount, will only lend above £15,000 in order not to be caught by the Act.

Very often, agreements will have a total repayment well in excess of £15,000 when all charges are taken into account. However, the significant figure for determining is *the fixed sum credit*. This means that it is the amount lent not the final figure payable Where the credit is what is known as "running account", meaning that the debtor has been given a pre-set credit limit by the creditor, the significant figure is the credit limit.

Running account and fixed sum credit are defined by section 109 of the Consumer Credit Act. Section 10(3) provides a little more protection for the person with the running account credit by saying that they are protected by the act if the amount that they can withdraw is less than £15,000 at a time.

The next important definition of a regulated agreement is that the agreement must either be restricted use credit or unrestricted use credit. If the debtors use to which he/she can put the credit is in some way restricted by the creditor, then the credit is restricted use.

Example

A finance company will only lend the money if a certain item or items are purchased with it. The lender is not free to take the cash.

When a purchaser uses a credit card to buy goods, then that card is restricted to that store or other stores which might take the card. This is therefore restricted credit.

The next, and perhaps the most significant definition of whether or not a contract is regulated is that of whether the agreement is a debtor-creditor-supplier agreement or a debtor-creditor agreement. Generally speaking, the debtor achieves a much higher level of protection if his credit agreement can be classed as a debtor-creditor-supplier agreement.

Under the Consumer Credit Act, the word "supplier" means the person the debtor has legally contracted to obtain the goods or services from, not the person who actually hands them over. One example here is where the buyer obtains the goods on hire purchase and the finance company has bailed them out to him. The finance company is the supplier not the shop with whom the purchaser has been dealing.

On the basis of the above definitions, it can be seen that all credit agreements need to be categorised into:

a) price limits

b) fixed sum or running account credit

c) restricted use or unrestricted use credit

d) Debtor-creditor or debtor-creditor-supplier agreements

e) two or three party debtor-creditor-supplier agreements.

Agreements which are exempt

We need to look at agreements which are exempt under section 16 of the Consumer Credit Act. It is important that you understand these definitions, particularly if you are going to challenge an agreement.

The first four exemptions relate to land mortgages. Most first land mortgages are outside of the Act. A number of second mortgages not used to finance the purchase of land will fall into the Act.

Debtor-creditor-supplier agreements for running account credit where the debtor has to repay the balance in a single payment. These agreements are exempt from the Act. This is usually of most relevance where you have purchased a good using a card like American Express.

Debtor-creditor agreements where the cost of credit is very low are exempt. Very low is defined as meaning where the annual rate does not exceed 13% or 1% above the highest of any base rates published by the English and Scottish clearing banks.

Every other agreement where the sum loaned is less than £15,000 is a regulated agreement.

Withdrawing from an agreement

What the consumer will wish to know is: how can he/she get out of a credit agreement as cheaply as possible. Before we examine this question in more depth we should look a little closer at the licensing system.

Licensing

The Consumer Credit Act 1974 established a licensing system in an attempt to regulate the credit industry. This involves a system whereby licences can be issued to groups or individuals. Licences last for five years. An application for a licence can be refused or a licence can be suspended. Licences are required by:

a) anyone who lends money not in excess of £15,000 to individuals;

b) anyone who passes an individual on to a source of finance (a credit broker);

c) anyone who operates a credit reference agency;

d) anyone who gives consumer debt advice.

The penalties for operating without a licence are both civil and criminal. In relation to civil sanctions, if a lender attempts to enforce an agreement and that person has not got a licence then the agreement is unenforceable. It is always worth checking that the person has a licence, or company has a licence. In addition, if the credit broker is unlicensed but the creditor was licensed, once again the agreement is unenforceable without a validating order (Consumer Credit Act s 149).

Whenever a debtor wishes to escape an agreement then a check should always be made as to whether the broker is licensed. There is a register of licensed brokers kept in London.

Control of agreements

The Consumer Credit Act also controls agreements. The Act sets out the form that agreements should take. In addition, the Act also regulates the look of the agreement, such as colour and size of print etc. in order to ensure that it is understood by the person signing it.

If the creditor fails to comply with the formalities, the agreement is said to be improperly executed. In this case, the agreement cannot be enforced against the debtor without a court order.

Sections 60 and 61 of the Act enable regulations to be made to ensure that the debtor is aware of his/her obligations and rights. In particular, credit agreements should make clear the amount and timing of repayments, the Annual Percentage rate (APR) and the protection and remedies available to the debtor under the Act. The Act also sets out how many copies of the agreement the debtor should have.

The initial stages of a credit agreement, when a person completes the forms detailing income etc. amount to an *unexecuted agreement*. In this situation, the purchaser must be given a copy of what it is he/she has signed. When the deal is accepted by the finance company, a copy of the executed agreement must be sent to the debtor.

If instant credit is offered and everything is done on the spot, then the agreement is executed and offered and the debtor will have one copy at the outset.

Therefore, when the agreement is unexecuted the debtor receives two copies of the agreement, one at the outset and one on final execution. If the agreement is executed at the outset then the debtor will receive one copy.

Cancellable agreements

Consumers have the right, in most cases, to cancel credit agreements within a certain time.

In the case of a cancellable agreement changes are made to the provisions covering copies:

a) every copy must contain a notice in the prescribed form, telling the debtor of the right of cancellation, how to exercise it, and to whom it should be sent;

b) in cases where a second copy is required (i.e. where the agreement is unexecuted at the outset) the second copy must be sent by post so that no pressure is put on the debtor;

c) in cases where a second copy is not required then if the agreement is cancellable a notice detailing the cancellation rights must be sent through the Post to the debtor within seven days.

In the case of a cancellable agreement, if the requirements of a) above and b) and c) are not complied with, the unenforceability sanction is very severe, i.e. the creditor will be unable to enforce the agreement.

Other ways to withdraw

One of the cheapest ways of escaping from an agreement is to argue that there is no agreement in existence between the seller and buyer, that offer and acceptance has not occurred. This relates to the receipt of an unexecuted and executed agreement.

The final cheap way of escaping from an agreement is that of cancellation. The first step is to determine whether or not it is cancellable. Normally, where offer and acceptance has occurred, the agreement is binding on both parties. However, there is one escape route provided by Section 67 of the Consumer Credit Act.

By section 67, where oral representations have taken place in antecedent negotiations in the debtors presence and the agreement has been signed away from the trade premises of the creditor, the negotiator (i.e. the supplier or credit broker) or a party to a linked transaction, then the agreement is cancellable. Thus, if the buyer is allowed to take the agreement home and sign it then the agreement is cancellable.

Antecedent negotiations as defined by section 56 of the Consumer Credit Act includes anything said about the goods or credit by the creditor or the credit broker or the supplier in the debtors presence. Telephone negotiations are not covered as it is easy for the debtor to merely put the phone down.

Cancellation or cooling off period

As has been discussed, if the agreement was unexecuted the buyer should receive through the post within seven days the executed copy. Both the first and second copy should contain notice of cancellation rights. If the agreement was executed at the outset then a second notice of cancellation rights should be sent by post within seven days.

It is the receipt of the second copy or notice that begins the cooling off period. This period is five days following the day the second copy or notice is received.

The aim of cancellation is to restore the parties to the position they would have been in had the agreement never been concluded. Goods are returned and money handed back.

If there is a part exchange involved, particularly where motor vehicles are concerned, then under section 73, once the debtor has cancelled the agreement, the negotiator (credit broker or supplier) must hand back the part exchange car or its monetary value within 10 days.

Defective goods purchased on credit

The consumers recourse to change of goods or money back will lie with whomever he/she has the agreement. We have seen that the business with whom the purchaser has the contract will be liable under the various Acts for defective goods.

Unable to meet repayments

The first action here should be for the consumer to try to reach an agreement with the creditor. The creditor, when making a decision will be influenced by a number of factors, such as the saleability of the goods.

The type of credit agreement must be considered here. If the agreement is a loan the main principle is that it must be repaid. The only escape route, or breathing space for the debtor is that time to repay may be given.

If the agreement is a hire purchase or conditional sale agreement, then the finance company has legal title to the goods and one of the options open to the debtor who does not wish to keep the goods is to exercise his rights to terminate under section 99-100 of the Consumer Credit Act. This is a costly option. For termination to operate under section 99:

a) the agreement must be regulated under the Consumer Protection Act;

b) the goods are available at any time before the final payment becomes due;

c) all arrears must be paid;

d) the debtor is liable to pay the creditor half of the total price.

Below are two examples to illustrate the above:

Example 1

M buys a Computer for a total price of £3,000 in August 1995. This figure includes a deposit of £850 and interest charges of £700. The balance is repayable over 24 months at £89.58 a month. M pays two instalments in August and September and then is made redundant and falls into arrears. M visits you in December, then 2 months in arrears. One of M's options is to terminate the agreement. as the total price is £3000, the starting half point figure is £1500. M has paid £179.16 and thus there is £1320.84 to pay including the arrears. M has to clear the arrears but in section 100(3) there is a provision that states that if a case does come to court, then if the court is satisfied that a sum less than one half would be equal to the loss suffered by the creditor then it may order a lesser amount. M can try to argue that because the finance company is receiving almost new goods back quickly, paying them the two months arrears should satisfy them.

Example 2

L purchases a car on a conditional sale agreement for a total price of £12,500 including interest charges. He gives a £1600 deposit leaving the balance repayable over 30 months of £363.33. After 12 months he loses his job and falls into arrears. He visits you for advice after three months arrears have accrued. In this case, the total price is £12500, half being £6250. He has paid £5000 plus £1600 giving a total of £6500. Therefore, if he clears his arrears then he can terminate, ending his liability.

The above examples have been based on the fact that the consumer may wish to keep the goods. There may be a situation where the debtor might want to hang on to the goods. This also depends on the type of the credit agreement. If the agreement is a loan then it must be repaid. The goods purchased are the debtors and can be sold to repay the loan. If a debtor gets into any kind of financial difficulties then a default notice will be served on him by the finance company. This notice must be served before any further action can be taken. At least seven days must be given to remedy the breach. The debtor, in response can, if he wishes apply to the court for a time order. This gives more time to pay off arrears.

The debtor can also retain goods by making them "protected". This means, basically, that the finance company, or whoever owns the goods will have to obtain a court order before the goods can be seized. This take time and the debtor will gain longer to pay off debts owed.

The Consumer Credit Act also provides that goods are protected if the debtor has paid more than one third of the total price, the debtor is in breach of the agreement, the agreement is still valid and the property is owned by the creditor. If the creditor does seize the goods back without a court order, the agreement is terminated and the debtor can obtain all money paid to date as a refund.

The Consumer Credit Act and "Extortionate credit bargains"

This is a fairly new concept, having been introduced into the Consumer Credit Act in 1978. The extortionate credit bargains provisions apply even if the credit exceeds £15,000. The Act (s138) states that a bargain is extortionate if it requires the debtor to make payments which are grossly exorbitant. The concept of grossly exorbitant will take into account interest rates prevailing at the time of the transaction and also other factors such as the relationship of the creditor with the debtor. The debtor can take proceedings through the county court to have the bargain re-examined and reopened.

The position of hired goods

There has been a marked increase in the incidence of hired goods during the last ten years. This is partly to do with the cyclical nature of our economy and the fact that it is quite often cheaper to hire goods than to buy them. In addition, if a person needs an expensive good, such as a floor sander, for a few days only then it is obviously cheaper to rent than buy.

The Sale of Goods Act does not cover hired items as there has been no transfer of goods. However, Part 1 of the 1982 Supply of Goods Act covers hired goods. Exclusion notices are covered by the Unfair Contract Terms Act, section 7

Section 101 0f the Supply of Goods Act 1982 governs the right of the hirer to terminate the agreement after 18 months, even if the hire period was longer. All money due within the 18 months must be paid

Key points from Chapter 2

* The most important Act dealing with consumers and credit is the Consumer Credit Act 1974

* There are a number of common types of credit agreements which are regulated by the CCA 1974, e.g. hire purchase, credit cards etc.

* Credit not exceeding £15,000 is regulated by the Act

* The Consumer Credit Act operates within a system of licences granted to finance companies and business generally

CHAPTER THREE

THE TRADE DESCRIPTIONS ACT

We have all seen goods that are described in weird and wonderful ways and yet, when we actually examine the good it is nothing special and does not match up to what we were led to believe.

The 1968 Trade Descriptions Act regulates the way business can describe their products. Section 1(1) states that any person who, in the course of a trade or business:

a) applies a false trade description to any goods; or

b) supplies or offers to supply any goods to which a false trade description is applied shall be guilty of an offence.

Section 2 of the Act lists 10 ways in which a trade description can be applied. These cover most eventualities. The most common offences are related to the motor industry, in particular to second hand cars and the falsifying of mileage.

Breach of the Trade Descriptions Act is a criminal offence. The maximum fine is usually no higher than £5,000. However, persistent breach of trade description, with a direct attempt to falsify, can lead to imprisonment.

Breach of the Trade Descriptions Act is only committed by someone in the course of business. Private individuals are not usually covered by the Act. Some traders will try to avoid liability by disclaiming-i.e., issuing a disclaimer notice. The issuing of disclaimers is subject to many restrictions. In order to be effective the disclaimer must have been issued before the trader supplied the goods. Sentences in small print are ineffective and general notices are also redundant.

Even if a trader complies with the above then if it is seen that the issue of a disclaimer is an attempt to avoid liability, in the full knowledge that a good is, or may be, defective, then a trader will still be liable.

Counterfeit goods

Counterfeit goods have caused problems, particularly in recent years. There are other Acts, such as Trade Marks Act 1938 or Copyright Designs and Patents Act 1988 which can prevent traders from passing off imitations as the real thing. Typical imitations are substituting imitation Levi's or watches.

If , however, you are sold a product and receive no notice that it is not the real thing, then subsequently discover that it is an imitation, then you can sue under the Trade Descriptions Act.

Services

The supply of services is covered by section 14 of the Trade Descriptions Act. Section 14 states that:

..It shall be an offence for any person in the course of trade or business to make a statement which he knows to be false or recklessly to make a statement which is false as to services, accommodation or facilities. This has been particularly relevant to holidays in recent years. Holiday companies make all sorts of promises and when the unsuspecting holidaymaker arrives abroad, they are often horrified to discover that the hotel is completely lacking in facilities claimed and their holidays are ruined.

Section 14 of the Act, as we have seen states that it is an offence for the person in the course of trade to "knowingly" or "Recklessly" make a statement which is false. Therefore, it is necessary to prove that what was said was a deliberate lie, or was said recklessly and, even though not intended to deceive, led to that a breach of the Trade Descriptions Act.

Holiday companies are now also regulated by a European Directive, the Package Travel package Holidays and Package Tours Regulations 1992. These regulations create a civil and criminal liability and apply to all packages sold in the United Kingdom after December 31st 1992. The regulations create strict guidelines and have closed many loopholes. The Regulations cover price, accommodation, information. Liability for damages is also defined more clearly. The Department of Trade and Industry have a leaflet available which expands on the obligations of the tour industry.

Defences to a Trade Descriptions Claim

Section 24 of the Trade Descriptions Act states that it shall be a defence for the person charged to prove that:

a) that the commission of the offence was due to a mistake, or to reliance on information supplied to him, or to the act or default of another person, an accident, or some other cause beyond his control; and

b) that he took all reasonable precautions and exercised all due diligence to avoid the commission of such an offence by himself or any person under his control.

The courts will demand clear evidence from a supplier before accepting either of the above as a defence.

CHAPTER FOUR

THE CONSUMER AND
UNSAFE GOODS

Sometimes the consumer purchases a good which, when tested turns out to be unsafe. If a contract exists between the consumer and retailer then the Sale of Goods Act s14 will give protection. If no such contract exists then the Consumer Protection Act 1987 will apply. The Consumer Protection Act also provides for criminal liability.

The Consumer Protection Act is not aimed at shoddy goods, but at unsafe goods. The Act sets out a general offence of supplying consumer goods which are not reasonably safe, provides for safety regulations to be made for products and provides for a system of notices to assist trading standards officers to enforce the Act.

Many consumer goods are controlled, or the safety of goods is controlled by detailed regulations related to the manufacture of a particular good. However, the Consumer Protection Act provides for a general safety standard.

Section 19 of the Act defines what is "safe" and states:

"Safe in relation to any goods means that there is no risk, or no risk apart from one reduced to a minimum". Therefore, goods do not have to be 100 safe. This is probably an impossibility. However, the risk of unsafe goods must be reduced to a minimum.

A person is guilty of an offence if he supplies any consumer goods which fail to comply with the general safety requirement, offers or agrees to supply any such good or exposes or possesses any such goods for supply.

Section 10 (1) and (2) are the relevant sections of the Act and section 10(2) contains a list of factors to be taken into account.

There are, as with all areas of law, recognised defences to the supply of unsafe goods. The important ones are:

a) the goods conform in a relevant respect with a European Community obligation;

b) the goods conform to any applicable safety regulations or safety standards set out by the Secretary of State for Trade and Industry for the purpose of the general safety requirement

c) that the offenders reasonably believed that the goods would not be used or consumed in the United Kingdom;

d) that the goods were supplied in the course of a business and that at the time the retailer did not know or had no reasonable grounds for believing that the goods failed to comply with the general safety requirements.;

e) that the goods were not supplied as new. The general safety requirement does not apply to second hand goods.

Penalties for contravention of the law can be up to £5,000 fine or six months in prison. However, this can vary greatly and a trader on trial for manslaughter can expect a higher sentence.

The European Community has been very active in this area and the current position is that a General Product Safety Directive has been issued to standardise the safety of food throughout Europe .

Key Points Chapter 4

* If a contract exists between the consumer and retailer, then the Sale of Goods Act s14 will give protection

* If no such contract exists then the Consumer Protection Act will apply

CHAPTER FIVE

THE SAFETY OF FOOD

Food poisoning is an increasing problem in our society and in the last decade there has been a massive increase in the number of reported cases. The major protection for the consumer in this area is the *1990 Food Safety Act*. The aim of the Act is to control all aspects of food safety throughout the food distribution chain. Breaches of the Act result in criminal liability. There is an unlimited fine attached to breaches of the Act and also a maximum prison term of two years.

Section 7 of the 1990 Food Safety Act creates a specific offence of rendering food injurious to health with the intent that it should be sold for human consumption. The offence can be committed in several ways:

a) by adding any article or substance to the food

b) by using any article or substance as an ingredient in the preparation of food

c) abstracting any constituent from the food;

d) subjecting the food to any other process or treatment.

Section 8 of the Act also creates a number of offences and states:

"Any person who sells for human consumption or offers, exposes or advertises for sale for such consumption or has in his possession for the purpose of such sale or of preparation for such sale any food which fails to comply with food safety requirements shall be guilty of an offence"

Food can be unfit for human consumption even if it poses no health hazard. For example, this is relevant to food which has started to incur mould growth.

The Food Safety Act also deals with food which misleads consumers. Section 14 states that anyone who sells food which is, by substance, not of the nature and quality demanded by the consumer is guilty of an offence, namely that of misleading the consumer. There are many examples here, particularly concerning meat and meat substitutes, i.e., fat instead of mince and fish. Section 15 of the Act Deals with the labelling of food and attempts to mislead by false claims.

The Act also contains many powers for food inspectors to inspect and seize food and to close down premises.

There are, as with the other areas of law, defences to breaches of the Act. One main defence is that of due diligence. However, in common with the other areas, defences have to be sound and backed up with concrete evidence.

Key points Chapter 5

* The 1990 Food Safety Act regulates food safety generally

* Breaches of the Act result in criminal liability

CHAPTER SIX

CONTROL OF PRICES

Many consumers find themselves in the position of thinking that they have a bargain and when it comes to paying for the good find that the price is higher than they thought.

Part 3 of the Consumer Protection Act 1987 controls, or regulates prices. The Act makes it a criminal offence to give consumers a misleading price indication about goods or services or accommodation. However, the Act only creates a general offence. It empowers the Secretary of State to approve a code of practice setting out guidelines for retailers as to the practice that they ought to follow. The Act does not actually require the retailer to follow the code.

The important fact is that it is only a code of practice. The term "Misleading" is defined in section 21 of the Act and covers indications about any conditions attached to a price, about future prices, price comparisons, as well as indications about the actual price the consumer will have to pay. The Act is enforced by the local Trading Standards Officers. The following guidance is given to retailers in the Code:

Price comparisons

a) the higher price as well as the price the retailer intends to charge should always be stated. Therefore, £5 reduced to £3 is good, but sale price £6 is misleading

b) in any comparison between the present selling price and another price, the previous price as well as the new lower price should be stated.

c) the product should have been available to consumers for at least 28 consecutive days in the last six months and in the same shop where the reduced price is being offered. If not, then this should be made clear

d) general disclaimers should not be used but specific stores and prices should be referred to.

Again, this is a code of guidance and retailers do not have to follow it. However, the retail industry is attempting to be self regulating.

Introductory Offers

a) an introductory offer should not be described as such unless it is intended to charge a higher price later

b) an introductory offer should not be allowed to run overlong

c) future increased prices can be quoted e.g. "our price now, until next year is £250. After this period it will be £480.

Comparison to prices related to different circumstances

The most common guidelines here are:

a) For goods in a totally different state, e.g. goods in a kit form as opposed to assembled

b) reductions for pensioners on certain days. These must be expressed in such a way that consumers are not misled and the goods or services must be available at the higher price.

References to worth or value

Price comparisons with another traders prices are allowed

Statements should not be made along the lines of "if you can buy for less we will refund the difference" unless the offer applies to another traders equivalent goods.

Actual price to the consumer

The Act makes it an offence to indicate a price for goods or services which is lower than the one that actually applies. Extras such as delivery charges and postage must be clearly indicated.

Service charges

These should be stated if they are non optional and should be incorporated in the price if possible or practicable. Extra non optional charges can be made but these must be drawn to the customers attention.

Price Marking

The Price Marking Order 1991, made under **the 1974 Prices Act** implements two European Directives concerning prices, one in relation to food and the other in relation to non food products. This states that the selling price and, in certain cases, the unit price of goods which may be for sale by retail must be indicated in writing. Guidance is given to retailers as to where the price should be shown.

Key Points Chapter 6

* The Consumer Protection Act 1987 controls, or regulates prices

* It is a criminal offence to give consumers a misleading price indication about goods, services or accommodation

* Although a general offence is created, there is no specific requirement for retailers to abide by the law

66

CHAPTER SEVEN

THE CONSUMERS REMEDIES

There are a number of remedies available to the consumer. The Principal remedy is through the civil courts-more specifically the small claims court, which is part of the county court. What follows is a description of the small claims procedure and of remedies available to the aggrieved consumer. Following this there will be a description of other remedies, such as the Office of Fair Trading.

The Small Claims Court

The first fact to be aware of when taking a trader to court in order to obtain some sort of compensation is that it is not necessary to have either legal knowledge or use a solicitor when using the small claims procedure in the County Court.

The procedure is designed so that remedies are available to the public at large without having to resort to expensive legal help.

It is the local court which decides private disputes and generally the small claims limit is £3,000. The county court is not a criminal court and is separate from the Crown Court and the Magistrates Court.

There are about 300 county courts in England and Wales and you should be able to find one within easy reach of your home. Alternatively, the local Citizens Advice Bureau or Consumer Advice Centre can give you the address of the court.

A few examples of claims for under £3,000 which can be made in the county court are:

a) Payment for failure to pay for goods sold

b) Compensation for faulty service by a garage, builder, dry cleaner or similar business

c) Claims against sellers of faulty goods

d) Disputes between landlord and tenant.

e) Claims against other road drivers

However, it is more specifically grievances concerning consumer goods that we are concerned with here.

Limitation periods

The law imposes time limits, known as limitation periods within which you must commence your case. Time begins to run from the date of the breach of contract. In personal injury cases it runs from the date when the injury was sustained or, if it is later from the date when the plaintiff first knew of their injuries. The court has a discretion to extend the time available in personal injury cases in certain circumstances.

The time limits are:

Contract	3 years
Tort	6 years
Defective products (Consumer Protection Act 1987)	3 years
Personal injury	3 years

Prevent claims Arising

Obviously it is highly desirable to avoid litigation if at all possible and the best way to do this is to prevent claims arising.

If you are a consumer and intend to employ someone to perform a service obtain estimates beforehand outlining exactly what is to be done and how much it will cost. It is also wise to ask if the people you are doing business with belong to any professional or trade associations. Write and confirm all the details of the contract before the work begins.

Ensure that you keep all relevant documents, such as a receipt for a payment, the contract guarantees, delivery note or any letters written. Also keep a copy of any advertisement you relied on in entering into a contract. If you speak to anyone on the telephone, make a record of the persons name and of what was said. A case often turns on the documentary evidence available at the arbitration hearing and relevant documents with which you may have to use to prove a case to the satisfaction of a judge usually come into existence before or during a dispute.

Steps you should take before taking legal action

The small claims court should be viewed as a last resort. Before issuing a Summons, make a clear complaint and attempt to reach a compromise by contacting the defendant. If no compromise or settlement is achieved, before issuing a Summons, you should write to the defendant threatening legal action and stating the recompense you are demanding. This is known as a letter before action. It is important to keep a copy of this and of all correspondence.

You may decide you would like to try and negotiate a compromise or make an offer of settlement.

Procedure

When a county court summons for £3,000 or less is issued, the dispute is categorised as a "small claim" and is automatically referred by the Court to "Arbitration". This in an informal procedure where a Judge hears each side of a dispute in a private room, rather than in an Open Court. Solicitors fees are not awarded to the successful party to an automatic Arbitration - unlike a hearing in Open Court. This is to encourage members of the public to conduct their own case.

The Court provides standard forms for completion by the opponents throughout a case with the intention that for simple matters, you could present your own case.

Clearly, you might be in a stronger position and feel more confident if you employed a Solicitor to present your case, but be aware that if you win, you will not be entitled to recover your legal costs. The small claims procedure is designed for self-representation.

The steps you must take to begin a County Court action against another person(s) are as follows:

Issue a Summons

A summons is a document which is used to start proceedings in the County Court. In small claims cases it is a form which the Plaintiff fills in. A summons form can be obtained from the Court Office. When you have completed the form two copies of the Summons must be taken to the Court Office and the Court Fee paid. The court will then serve (i.e. post) the Summons on the Defendant with three forms, a Form of Admission

(N9A), a form for filing a Defence (N9B) and a form for filing a Counterclaim (N9B). The Court will also:

*   post a form called a "Plaint Note" (N205A) to you. This form records the details of the claim, the case number and date of service. The case number is now the reference point for your case and no steps can be taken without quoting it

*   you will also receive a Request for Judgement which is attached to the Plaint Note.

To claim damages two types of Summons are available, they are:

*   a Summons claiming a fixed sum of money, known as a "liquidated demand" - Form N1, or

*   a Summons claiming damages to be assessed, where the court must assess and determine the level of compensation payable - Form N2.

Court Service. The court will post the Summons to the Defendant with a Form of Admission, Defence and Counterclaim.

The Summons used in small claims is described as a "Default Summons". This is a summons used to start a "default action". The significance of the term "default" is that, if the Defendant does not file a defence, the court will order judgement in the Plaintiff's favour without a hearing. In other words, by issuing a default summons, the Defendant is summonsed to answer the Plaintiff's claim and if he fails to do so by not filing a defence, the court will order judgement for the Plaintiff. In the case of a claim for a fixed amount, the court will order payment of that amount. If the amount is not specified, the court will order judgement for the Plaintiff with damages to be assessed. A hearing date will be set for the assessment of damages.

Defence

If the Defendant files a Defence, the Plaintiff will receive a copy from the Court and the case will be transferred to the Defendant's local court which will set a date for the Arbitration Hearing. If you are a Plaintiff and you expect the Defendant to file a defence, you will save time if you issue your Summons in his local County Court. If a Defence is not filed within 14 days of service, the Plaintiff may return the Request for Judgement, and Judgement-in-Default will be entered in his favour. He will then receive a copy of the Judgement which will be in the form of an order for immediate payment or payment by instalments.

Counterclaim

The Defendant's counterclaim is a claim made by the Defendant against the Plaintiff which may be less than his claim, so his claim is reduced, or it may be greater. A counterclaim is a separate action. Rather than the Defendant issuing his own Summons, the dispute is managed in one set of proceedings by the defendant issuing a counterclaim. The Plaintiff is entitled to file a defence to the counterclaim. However, the Plaintiff is treated as having denied the allegations made in a counterclaim if a defence is not filed. Judgement-in-default is therefore not applicable to a counterclaim.

Date of the Arbitration Hearing

If a defence is filed, the court will set a date for the arbitration and issue directions - you will be notified by Form N18A. The Court must

*   give not less than 14 days notice of the date of the hearing, and

*   issue directions before any hearing or pre-hearing.

Enforcement Proceedings

If the Defendant does not comply with the Judgement, which is a Court Order, you will be entitled to take enforcement proceedings.

What to do Next

Take the two copies of the completed summons form to the court and pay the issue fee. Remember to keep a copy for yourself. The court may ask for copies. The court will stamp the summons form and post it to the defendant with forms of admission, defence and counterclaim, explained in the next chapter. The defendant must reply to your summons within 14 days from the date of service printed on the Plaint Note. A company has 16 days to reply.

If the Defendant files a defence, the court will post a copy to you. A form of Admission is returned direct to the Plaintiff.

THE COSTS OF ARBITRATION

<u>County Court Fees</u>

These are fees which must be paid to the court to commence and enforce your claim. These should be checked with the county court.

You do not have to pay court fees if you are receiving income support at the time the fee is paid. This exemption applies even if you are receiving legal advice and assistance under the "Green form Scheme" but not if you are in receipt of legal representation under Part IV of the Legal Aid Act 1988 for the purpose of proceedings. You may also be exempt from paying fees, at the discretion of the Chief Clerk, if you can show that paying the fee would cause undue hardship because of the exceptional circumstances of the case.

Recovering Costs From Your Opponent

Small claims are an exception to the usual practice where in general if you win your case your opponent pays you costs. In small claims even if you are entirely successful only a few of your possible expenses will be recoverable. They are:

The costs which were stated on the summons or which would have been on the summons if the claim had been for a liquidated sum.

Up to £200 in respect of the fees of an expert. Inclusive of VAT.

Up to £260 for legal advice obtained to bring or defend a claim for an injunction, specific performance or similar relief. Inclusive of VAT.

Up to £50 in respect of a party's or a witness's loss of earnings when attending a hearing.

Any expenses which have been reasonably incurred by a party or a witness in travelling to and from the hearing or in staying away from home.

The costs of enforcing the award.

Such further costs as a district judge may direct where there has been unreasonable conduct on the part of the opposite party in relation to the proceedings or a claim that was made. An example of unreasonable conduct would be the fabrication of a wholly untruthful defence.

Legal Aid

The Legal Aid green form scheme is available to pay for a limited amount of advice and assistance from a solicitor for those with sufficiently low incomes. It does not cover representation at the hearing or court fees but might provide payment for expert evidence. Consult a solicitor for advice about whether or not you are eligible under the green form scheme.

The Legal Aid Board's guidance on the availability of ordinary legal aid (non-green form scheme), which could include representation at the hearing, suggests that it should not be granted within the small claims procedure "unless there are exceptional circumstances and there will be a tangible benefit to an assisted person". If you think you might be eligible consult a solicitor for advice. You should bear in mind that if you do receive legal aid there will be a statutory charge. This means that the costs you incur will be paid out of any damages or compensation you receive and you will only be able to keep what is left over.

ENFORCING THE JUDGEMENT

Once you have obtained judgement on the claim or counterclaim no further action is required so long as the damages are paid. However debtors do not always comply with the court's order to pay a lump sum and may fall into arrears with payments to be made by instalments, in which case you have a number of options and can ask the court for any of the following:

Warrant of Execution

This gives bailiffs the authority to seize goods to the value of the debt

Attachment of earnings order

This gives the court the authority to take the total of the debt from the debtors bank account

Garnishee Order

This is an order which freezes the bank account of the debtor until the debt has been paid.

Charging Order/order for sale

This is an order which is attached to property, stocks and bonds etc.

Oral Examination

This is where the court orders the debtor to attend court and submit to an examination of means, in order to determine what the debtor can feasibly pay of the debt owed.

Bankruptcy

This is where the creditor can apply for the company/person to be made bankrupt.

In all the cases above, there will be appropriate guidance in the county court.

The court will advise of the most appropriate enforcement remedy.

Other remedies

Many retailers belong to trade associations, for example the Society of Motor Manufacturers and Traders. There are also Codes of Practice governing various industries, for example ABTA for the holiday and tourist industry. In many cases, redress can be obtained through these associations which can help you bypass the sometimes long and drawn out small claims procedure.

Many consumers report their complaints to their local Trading Standards Officer. Detailed figures are passed on to the office of fair trading in London. The 1973 Fair Trading Act enables the Director General of Fair Trading to begin procedures to halt practices which are harmful to consumers and to pursue individual traders whom it is believed have engaged in unfair practice.

Assurances under the Fair Trading Act

Sections 34-42 of the Fair Trading Act give the Director General Power to act against someone who in the course of business continually acts in a way which is to the detriment of consumers.

APPENDIX 1

Example 1

PARTICULARS OF CLAIM

1.The Defendants are and were at all material times in the business of selling car cleaning products.

2.On the 7th February 1996 the Defendants in the course of the said business contracted with the Plaintiff and sold 5 bottles of detergent at a price of £192

3.At the time of the said contract the Plaintiff told the Defendants that the said detergent would be used for the purpose of cleaning the plaintiffs car.

4.It was an implied term of the said contract that the said detergent should be :

a) reasonably fit for the said purpose

b) of satisfactory quality.

5.On the 10th February the Plaintiff used the said detergent to clean his car

6.In breach of the said implied terms the said detergent was not fit for the required purpose and was not of satisfactory quality in that it damaged the plaintiff's car beyond repair. The said car lost its colour and developed patches on the paintwork.

7.By reason of the matters aforesaid the Plaintiff has suffered loss and damage.

PARTICULARS OF DAMAGE

1) Value of car

                       £11,000

2) Cost of respray   £2,000

,

AND the plaintiff claims

1)   Damages

2)   Interest

3)   Costs

Appendix 2 Key forms used in the county court

1. Default Summons N1

2. Default summons-unspecified amount N2

3. Notice of issue of default summons and request for judgement N205A

4. Notice of Arbitration hearing and judges directions N18A

N1 Default summons

County Court Summons

Case Number

In the

County Court

(1)

Plaintiff's
full name
address

(2)

Address for
service (and)
payment
(if not as above)
Ref/Tel no.

Telephone:

Seal

(3)

Defendant's
name
address

This summons is only valid if sealed by the court
If it is not sealed it should be sent to the court

What the plaintiff claims from you

Brief
description
of type of
claim

Particulars of the plaintiff's claim against you

Amount claimed

Court fee

Solicitor's costs

Total amount

Summons issued on

What to do about this summons

You can

- **dispute the claim**
- **make a claim against the plaintiff**
- **admit the claim in full and offer to pay**
- **pay the total amount shown above**
- **admit only part of the claim**

**For information on what to do or if you
need further advice, please turn over.**

Signed
Plaintiff's solicitor)
(or see enclosed particulars of claim)

N1 Default summons (fixed amount) (Order 3, rule 3(2)(b))

Keep this summons, you may need to refer to it

N1 continued

You have 21 days from the date of the postmark to reply to this summons

(A limited company served at its registered office has 16 days to reply.)

If you do nothing	Judgment may be entered against you without further notice.
If you dispute the claim	Complete the white defence form (N9B) and return it to the court office. The notes on the form explain what you should do.
If you want to make a claim against the plaintiff (counterclaim)	Complete boxes 5 and 6 on the white defence form (N9B) and return the form to the court office. The notes at box 5 explain what you should do.
If you admit all of the claim and you are asking for time to pay	Fill in the blue admission form (N9A). The notes on the form explain what you should do and where you should send the completed form.
If you admit all of the claim and you wish to pay now	Take or send the money to the person named at box (2) on the front of the summons. If there is no address in box (2), send the money to the address in box (1). Read How to Pay below.
If you admit only part of the claim	Fill in the white defence form (N9B) saying how much you admit, then either: Pay the amount admitted as explained in the box above; or Fill in the blue admission form (N9A) if you need time to pay

Interest on Judgments

If judgment is entered against you and is for more than £5000, the plaintiff may be entitled to interest on the total amount.

Registration of Judgments

If the summons results in a judgment against you, your name and address may be entered in the Register of County Court Judgments. This may make it difficult for you to get credit. A leaflet giving further information can be obtained from the court.

Further Advice

You can get help to complete the reply forms and information about court procedures at any county court office or citizens' advice bureau. The address and telephone number of your local court is listed under "Courts" in the phone book. When corresponding with the court, please address forms or letters to the Chief Clerk. Always quote the whole of the case number which appears at the top right corner on the front of this form; the court is unable to trace your case without it.

How to pay	To be completed on the court copy only
• PAYMENT(S) MUST BE MADE to the person named at the address for payment quoting their reference and the court case number.	Served on
• DO NOT bring or send payments to the court. THEY WILL NOT BE ACCEPTED.	By posting on
• You should allow at least 4 days for your payments to reach the plaintiff or his representative.	
• Make sure that you keep records and can account for all payments made. Proof may be required if there is any disagreement. It is not safe to send cash unless you use registered post.	Officer
• A leaflet giving further advice about payment can be obtained from the court.	Marked "gone away" on
• If you need more information you should contact the plaintiff or his representative.	

N2 Default summons unspecified amount

County Court Summons

Plaintiff's full name address

Case Number

In the

County Court

The court office is open from 10am to 4pm Monday to Friday

Plaintiff's Solicitor's address

Ref/Tel No.

Telephone

Defendant's full name (including title e.g. Mr, Mrs or Miss) **and address**

seal

This summons is only valid if sealed by the court. If it is not sealed it should be sent to the court.

Keep this summons, you may need to refer to it.

What the plaintiff claims from you

Give brief description of type of claim

Particulars of the plaintiff's claim against you

	Amount claimed	see particulars
Court fee		
Solicitor's costs		
Total Amount		

Summons issued on _____

What you should do

You have 21 days (16 days if you are a limited company served at your registered office) from the date of the postmark to either

- **defend the claim** by filling in the back of the enclosed form and **sending it to the court**;

OR

- **admit the claim** and make an offer of payment, by filling in the front of the enclosed reply form and **sending it to the court**.

If you do nothing judgment may be entered against you.

My claim is worth   £5000 or less ☐   over £5000 ☐

All cases over £1000

I would like my case decided by   trial ☐   arbitration ☐

Signed
Plaintiff or plaintiff's solicitor
(or see enclosed "Particulars of claim")

N2 Default summons (amount not fixed) Order 3. rule 3.2(1b)

N2 continued

Please read this page : it will help you deal with the summons

If you dispute all or part of the claim

You may be entitled to help with your legal costs. Ask about the legal aid scheme at any county court office, citizens' advice bureau, legal advice centre or firm of solicitors displaying the legal aid sign.

● Say how much you dispute in the part of the enclosed form for defending the claim and return it to the court. The court will tell you what to do next.

● If you dispute only part of the claim, you should also fill in the part of the form for admitting the claim and pay the amount admitted into court.

● If the court named on the summons is not your local county court, and/or the court for the area where the reason for the claim arose, you may write to the court named asking for the case to be transferred to the county court of your choice. You must explain your reasons for wanting the transfer . However, if the case is transferred and you later lose the case, you may have to pay more in costs.

How the claim will be dealt with if defended

If the claim is worth £1,000 or less it will be dealt with by arbitration (small claims procedure) unless the court decides the case is too difficult to be dealt with in this informal way. Costs and the grounds for setting aside an arbitration award are strictly limited. If the claim is for £1,000 or less and is not dealt with by arbitration, costs, including the costs of help from a legal representative, may be allowed.

If the claim is worth over £1000 it can still be dealt with by arbitration if either you or the plaintiff asks for it and the court approves. If your claim is dealt with by arbitration in these circumstances, costs may be allowed.

If you want to make a claim against the plaintiff

This is known as a counterclaim

Fill in the part of the enclosed form headed 'Counterclaim'. If your claim is for more than the plaintiff's claim you may have to pay a fee - the court will let you know. Unless the plaintiff admits your counterclaim there will be a hearing. The court will tell you what to do next.

If you admit the claim or any part of it

● You may pay an appropriate amount into court to compensate the plaintiff (see Payments Into Court box on this page), accompanied by a notice (or letter) that the payment is in satisfaction of the claim. If the plaintiff accepts the amount paid he is also entitled to apply for his costs.

● If you need time to pay, complete the enclosed form of admission and give details of how you propose to pay the plaintiff. If your offer is accepted, the court will send an order telling you how to pay. If it is not accepted, the court will fix a rate of payment based on the details given in your form of admission and the plaintiff's comments. Judgment will be entered and you will be sent an order telling you how and when to pay.

● If the plaintiff does not accept the amount paid or offered, the court will fix a hearing to decide how much you must pay to compensate the plaintiff. The court will tell

you when the hearing, which you should attend, will take place.

General information

● If you received this summons through the post the date of service will be 7 days (for a limited company at its registered office, the second working day) after the date of posting as shown by the postmark.

● You can get help to complete the enclosed form and information about court procedures at any county court office or citizens' advice bureau. The address and telephone number of your local court is listed under 'Courts' in the phone book.

● Please address forms or letters to the Chief Clerk.

● Always quote the whole of the case number which appears at the top right corner of the front of this form; the court is unable to trace your case without it.

Registration of Judgments

If the summons results in a judgment against you, your name and address may be entered in the Register of County Court Judgments. This may make it difficult for you to get credit. A leaflet giving further information can be obtained from the court.

Interest on Judgments

If judgment is entered against you and is for more than £5000, the plaintiff may be entitled to interest on the total amount.

Payments Into Court

You can pay the court by calling at the court office which is open 10 am to 4 pm Monday to Friday

You may only pay by:
- cash
- banker's or giro draft
- cheque supported by a cheque card
- cheque (unsupported cheques may be accepted, subject to clearance, if the Chief Clerk agrees)

Cheques and drafts must be made payable to HM Paymaster General and crossed.
Please bring this form with you.

By post
You may only pay by:
- postal order
- banker's or giro draft
- cheque (cheques may be accepted, subject to clearance, if the Chief Clerk agrees).

The payment must be made out to HM Paymaster General and crossed.
This method of payment is at your own risk.
And you must:
- pay the postage
- enclose this form
- enclose a self addressed envelope so that the court can return this form with a receipt

The court cannot accept stamps or payments by bank and giro credit transfers.

Note: You should carefully check any future forms from the court to see if payments should be made directly to the plaintiff

---

To be completed on the court copy only

Served on:

By posting on:

Officer:

This summons was returned by the Post Office marked 'Gone Away' on:

N5 Default summons (amount not fixed)

Notice of issue of default summons N205A

Notice of Issue of Default Summons - fixed amount

To the plaintiff ('s solicitor)

[blank box]

Your summons was issued today. The defendant has 14 days from the date of service to reply to the summons. If the date of postal service is not shown on this form you will be sent a separate notice of service (Form N222).
The defendant may either

- Pay you your total claim.
- Dispute the whole claim. The court will send you a copy of the defence and tell you what to do next.
- Admit that all the money is owed. The defendant will send you form of admission N9A. You may then ask the court to send the defendant an order to pay you the money owed by completing the request for judgment below and returning it to the court.
- Admit that only part of your claim is owed. The court will send you a copy of the reply and tell you what to do next.
- Not reply at all. You should wait 14 days from the date of service. You may then ask the court to send the defendant an order to pay you the money owed by completing the request for judgment below and returning it to the court.

In the	**WOOLWICH** County Court

The court office at
THE COURT HOUSE, POWIS STREET,
LONDON SE18 6JW.

Is open between 10 am & 4 pm Monday to Friday
Tel: 081-854 2127

Case Number	*Always quote this*	
Plaintiff *(including ref.)*		
Defendants		
Issue date		
Date of postal service		
Issue fee	£	

For further information please turn over

. . . .

Request for Judgment

- Tick and complete either A or B. Make sure that all the case details are given and that the judgment details at C are completed. Remember to sign and date the form. Your signature certifies that the information you have given is correct.
- If the defendant has given an address on the form of admission or which correspondence should be sent, which is different from the address shown on the summons, you will need to tell the court.

A ☐ **The defendant has not replied to my summons**
Complete all the judgment details at C. Decide how and when you want the defendant to pay. You can ask for the judgment to be paid by instalments or in one payment.

B ☐ **The defendant admits that all the money is owed**
Tick only one box below and return the completed slip to the court.

☐ **I accept the defendant's proposal for payment**
Complete all the judgment details at C. Say how the defendant intends to pay. The court will send the defendant an order to pay. You will also be sent a copy.

☐ **The defendant has not made any proposal for payment**
Complete all the judgment details at C. Say how you want the defendant to pay. You can ask for the judgment to be paid by instalments or in one payment. The court will send the defendant an order to pay. You will also be sent a copy.

☐ **I do NOT accept the defendant's proposal for payment**
Complete all the judgment details at C and say how you want the defendant to pay. Give your reasons for objecting to the defendant's offer of payment to the section overleaf. Return this slip to the court together with the defendant's admission N9A (or a copy). The court will fix a rate of payment and send the defendant an order to pay. You will also be sent a copy.

I certify that the information given is correct

Signed _____   Dated _____

In the	**WOOLWICH** County Court

Case Number	*Always quote this*	
Plaintiff		
Defendant		
Plaintiff's Ref.		

C Judgment details
I would like the judgment to be paid

☐ (forthwith) *only ask this box if you intend to enforce the order right away*
☐ (by instalments of £ _____ per month)
☐ (in full by _____)

Amount of claim as stated in summons (including interest at date of issue)	
Interest since date of summons (if any) Period _____ Rate _____ %	
Court fee shown on summons	
Solicitor's costs (if any) on issuing summons	
Sub Total	
Solicitor's costs (if any) on entering judgment	
Sub Total	
Deduct amount (if any) paid since issue	
Amount payable by defendant	

N205A Notice of issue (default summons) and request for judgment (Order 3, rule 2X.6(1), Order 9 rules 3 and 6)

HCR 6882704521442 11/91

85

N205A continued

-- Further information --

- The summons must be served within 4 months of the date of issue (or 6 months if leave to serve out of the jurisdiction is granted under Order 8, rule 2). In exceptional circumstances you may apply for this time to be extended provided that you do so before the summons expires.

- If the defendant does not reply to the summons or if he delivers an admission without an offer of payment you may ask for judgment. If you do not ask for judgment within 12 months of the date of service the action will be struck out. It cannot be reinstated.

- You may be entitled to interest if judgment is entered against the defendant and your claim is for more than £5000.

- You should keep a record of any payments you receive from the defendant. If there is a hearing or you wish to take steps to enforce the judgment, you will need to satisfy the court about the balance outstanding. You should give the defendant a receipt and payment in cash should always be acknowledged. You should tell the defendant how much he owes if he asks.

- You must inform the court IMMEDIATELY if you receive any payment before a hearing date or after you have sent a request for enforcement to the court.

Objections to the defendant's proposal for payment

Case Number

Notice of Arbitration hearing N18A

Notice of Arbitration Hearing	**In the**		
Plaintiff		**Woolwich**	
			County Court
	Case No. *Always quote this*		
Defendant	**Plaintiff's Ref.**		
	Date	6 March 1995	

To the plaintiff and defendant

1. Details of Hearing

This case is to be dealt with by arbitration under the small claims procedure. The notes overleaf tell you more about the hearing and what you need to do before it takes place.

The arbitration hearing will take place at **The Court House, 165-167 Powis Street, Woolwich, SE18 6JW.**

on , at

The time allowed for the arbitration is hours, minutes

If you do not attend, the **district Judge (the arbitrator)** may make decisions in your absence.

If you do not wish your case to be dealt with under the informal small claims procedure, you may apply to the court. You should use form N244 which you can get free from the court office. You must say why you object to your case being dealt with as a small claims case.

The court will give you an appointment at which the district Judge will consider your objections. If your case is not dealt with under the small claims procedure, costs may be allowed. That means, if you lose the case you may have to pay the other party's costs which may include the costs of help from a legal representative.

2. District Judge's Directions (What you should do)

(i) Not less than 14 days before the hearing, you must send the other party a copy of all the documents you have which you are going to use to prove your case.

(ii) Not less than 7 days before the hearing, you must send the court and the other party:
(a) a copy of any expert report you are going to use to prove your case and
(b) the name(s) and address(es) of any witness(es) you intend to use.

The court office at Woolwich County Court, The Court House, 165-167 Powis Street Woolwich SE18 6JW is open between 10 am and 4 pm Monday to Friday. When corresponding with the court, please address forms or letters to the Chief Clerk and quote the case number. Tel: 081 854 2127

Notice of arbitration hearing (small claims procedure) (Order 19, Rule 3)

N18A

87

N18A continued

3. Help and Advice

- You may find it helpful to get advice about your claim and the evidence you should produce at the hearing. Many solicitors will give up to half an hour's advice for a fixed fee of £5, or you may be entitled to advice under the Legal Advice and Assistance Scheme. If expert evidence would help to prove your claim, your local Citizens Advice Bureau may be able to suggest the name of a suitable person to provide a report. They may also offer more general advice and assistance.

- You may take someone with you to the hearing to speak for you. They cannot come to the hearing alone. This person is called a 'lay representative' and can be anyone you choose, for example, your husband or wife, a relative, friend, or advice worker.

- Some lay representatives may want to be paid for helping you. You should make sure you know exactly how much this will be. Consider carefully whether your claim is worth paying that amount. Remember, you will have to pay this yourself.

- You should also remember that some lay representatives who charge for their services may not belong to any professional body. This means that if you are dissatisfied with the way they handle your case, there may be no one to whom you can complain.

- Small claims leaflet number 6 ("A defence to my claim - what happens now?") and leaflet number 7 (An arbitration hearing - how do I prepare?) will give you more information about the hearing and what you have to do.

4. Notes on the arbitration hearing

- Arbitration is an informal way of dealing with a claim. The hearing is normally held in private.

- At the hearing the district judge (the arbitrator) will decide on the best way to:
  - identify the facts and matters in dispute, and
  - make sure you have a fair and equal opportunity to present your case.

- The strict rules of evidence will not apply. The arbitrator may take into account any evidence as long as it is fair to both parties to do so.

- If you do not attend the hearing, the arbitrator will normally deal with the case in your absence. But any documents you have sent to the court will be taken into account.

- If you have a lay representative, remember to give the arbitrator form Ex183 at the beginning of the hearing. (The arbitrator can tell your lay representative to leave if he thinks he or she is behaving badly).

- If you do not have anyone to speak on your behalf, you can ask the arbitrator to help by putting questions for you.

- At the end of the hearing, the arbitrator will tell you the decision and the reasons for it.

- The decision ('award') made at the hearing is normally final. You can apply to have it set aside, but the grounds (reasons) for doing so are very limited.

USEFUL ADDRESSES

Advertising Standards Authority
2-16 Torrington Place
London WC1E 7HN
Tel: 0171 580 5555

Association of British Launderers and Cleaners
Lancaster Gate House
319 Pinner Road
Harrow
Middlesex HA1 4HX

Tel: 0181 836 7755

Association of British Travel Agents
55-57 Newman Street
London W1P 4AH

Tel: 0171 637 2444

Association of Manufacturers of Domestic Electrical Appliances
AMDEA House
593 Hitchin Road
Stopsley
Luton Beds LU2 7UN

Association of Photographic Laboratories
9 Warwick Court
London WC1 R 5DJ

Tel: 0171 405 2762

British Institute of Professional Photography
Amwell End Ware
Herts SG12 9HN

British Insurance Association
Aldermary House
Queen Street
London EC4p 4JD

Tel: 0171 248 4477

British Insurance Brokers Association
130 Fenchurch Street
London EC3M 5DJ

0171 623 9043

British Standards Institution
2 Park Street
London W1A 2BS

0171 629 9000

Citizens Advice Bureau
Various throughout Country
listed in directory

Consumers Association
14 Buckingham Street
London WC2N 6DS

Tel: 0171 839 1222

Department of Commerce
Northern Ireland
Chichester House
64 Chichester Street
Belfast BT1 4JX

Tel: 01232 34488

Department of Trade
1 Victoria Street
London SW1H OET

Tel: 0171 215 7877

Regional Offices throughout the country

Design Council
28 Haymarket
London SW1 4DG

Tel: 0171 580 8433

Domestic Coal Consumers Association
Gavrelle House
2 Bunhill Row
London EC1Y 8LL

Tel: 0171 638 8914

Electricity Consumers Council
119 Marylebone Road
London NW1 5PY

Tel: 0171 636 5703

Footwear Distributors Association
Commonwealth House
1-19 New Oxford Street
London WC1A 1PA

Tel: 0171 409 0955

Glass and Glazing Federation
6 Mount Row
London W1Y 6DY

Tel: 0171 409 0545

Hearing Aid Council
40A Ludgate Hill
London EC4M 7DE

Tel: 0171 9226

Home Office
50 Queen Annes Gate
London SW1H 9AT

Tel: 0171 213 3000

Independent Broadcasting Authority
70 Brompton Road
London SW3 1EY

Tel: 0181 584 7011

Insurance Ombudsman Service
31 Southampton Row
London WC1B 5HJ

Tel: 0171 242 8613

The Law Society
113 Chancery Lane
London WC2A 1PL

Tel: 0171 242 1222

London Transport Passengers Committee
1 King Street
London WC2 8HN

Mail Order Publishers Authority
1 New Burlington Street
London W1X 1FD

Tel: 0171 437 0706

The Mail Order Traders Association of GB
25 Castle Street
Liverpool L2 4TD

Tel: 0151 227 4181

Ministry of Agriculture Fisheries and Food
Great Westminster House
Horseferry Rd
London SW1P2AE

Tel: 0181 216 6311

Motor Agents Association
73 Park Street
Bristol BS1 5PS

Tel: 01272 293232

National Association of Funeral Directors
57 Doughty Street
London WC1N 2NE

Tel: 0171 242 9388

National Association of Retail Furnishers
17-21 George Street
Croyden CR9 1TQ

Tel: 0181 680 8444

National Consumer Council
18 Queen Annes Gate
London SW1H 9AA

Tel: 0181 222 9501

National Housebuilding Council
58 Portland Place
London W1N 4BU

Tel: 0171 637 1248

National Pharmaceutical Association
Mallinson House
40-42 St Peters Street
St Albans
Herts AL1 3NT

Tel: 01727 32161

Office of Fair Trading
Field House
Breams Buildings
London EC4 1PR

Tel: 0171 242 2858

Photographic Dealers Association
84 Newman Street
London W1P 3LD

Tel: 0171 323 4641

Radio Electrical and Television Retailers Association
RETRA House
57-61 Newington Causeway
London SE1 6BE

Tel: 0181 403 1463

Scottish House Furnishers Association
203 Pitt Street
Glasgow
G2 4DB

Tel: 0141 332 6381

Scottish Motor Trade Association
3 Palmerston Place
Edingburgh EH12 5AQ

Tel: 0131 225 3643

Society of Motor Manufacturers and Traders
Forbes House
Halkin Street
London SW1X 7DS

Vehicle Builders and Repairers Association
Belmont House
Finkle Lane
Gilderstone
Leeds LS27 7TW